Food of The Forest

The Aranyakas way

AF516811

BlueRose ONE.com
Stories Matter

First Published in December 2022

ISBN: 978-93-5668-488-1

BLUEROSE PUBLISHERS
www.BlueRoseONE.com
info@bluerosepublishers.com
+91 8882 898 898

Cover Design:
Aman Sharma

Typographic Design:
Namrata Saini

Distributed by: BlueRose, Amazon, Flipkart

From the Forest to You.......A Gift of Love

To all those hands that have toiled to feed the world and continue to do so, my deepest gratitude to them.

A Note

Before I take you all on my journey into the magical and healing properties of nature, I would like to clarify a few things. This book is based on my personal journey and is not to be used as prescription or as an authority on the subject. Please do consult with your Ayurved / doctor in case of doubt.

My personal encounters may sound outlandish to some but these are purely my own experiences. The happenings and occurrences all took place at Mangaal in Netravali Goa.

I thank all the beings and the land at Netravali.

With grace and blessings I share my story…

About the Author

Minakshi Singh

Minakshi Singh did her schooling in Mumbai and then went to pursue a bachelor's degree in arts in Jai Hind College, Mumbai, India.

Thereafter, she started a handicraft brand called "Chunari" in Jaipur retailing out of the iconic Rambagh Palace Hotel, Rajasthan, India.

In 2015, Minakshi answered her innate and present "call to the wild" and ventured into the world of agriculture and farming and obtained a "PDC" under the renowned facilitator Ms. Clea Chandmal.

In 2016, after implementing her knowledge and practicing her craft, pro- bono on numerous small subsistence farms, she started off as a freelance consultant, catering to larger farmlands in South Goa and North Goa. Her healing touch helped them rejuvenate the soil, and cultivate nutritionally rich plants, keeping in mind the local eco system.

In 2020, Minakshi co –founded "Aranyakas – The Forest Dwellers" a brand established to elaborate and imbibe the knowledge of sustainable living through natural products for our mind, body and soul.

"Liberate yourself from yourself" is her mantra for success!

Lock Down Time

For years, I have yearned to learn more about medicinal plants and their healing effects on the body and mind. Alas, there was no one to teach me. I never lost hope though and managed to get books like 'Herbs That Heal' written by Bakru and 'Home Remedies'by T V Sairam. But this was not enough! I had a strong urge to learn and knew more was to come my way. My wonderful tenure in Ladakh had been completed. I was free once more, only to find myself back in the place from where I first began my journey as a farmer, in the forests of Mangaal.

"I have a small two week project for you" read Jay's whatsapp message to me, "identify the medicinal plants and its benefits, would you be interested?" Before I knew it, my fingers were punching the keypad with a big "YES.

Jay is a friend of mine who owns a large plantation in South Goa. His love for medicinal plants and other plants in general could be seen in his plantation at Mangaal. One hundred and fifty trees were already identified but there were more to go. Many of these trees were labelled but more research was needed. "Please find their botanical names, local names and which family they belong to" read Jay's e-mail. " And so I was back where it all began. The land and its loving people called for me again.

So there I was in the forests of Netravali which always felt like home to me. After settling in, I could easily connect with the land and its forest. Jay had emailed me the list of trees so it was easy for me to begin my work.

I rummaged through various sites for detailed information on different parts of the plant, their uses and how to make decoctions. Slowly but surely I managed to complete my deadline when the 'lock down' in Goa took place.

I took advantage of this time to meditate with these plants and connected with their energy. For the longest time, it's been my dream to learn and understand the medicinal wisdom of plants. The studies showed me we had many plants which were anti-cancer, anti bacterial, anti fungal and anti oxidant.

The village at Mangaal was situated in a remote area of Netravali and did not show any signs of lock down. All the workers would come down from their village to work on the plantation as they would on a normal day. It wasn't until our farm manager Amrid came down with a cold and fever that I became aware that no doctors were available. Amrid is the whole and soul backbone of the farm. His falling ill would spell disaster. I panicked! 'Think, think, think,' I said to myself. This was also at the time where, on mere suspicion, people were picked up and put in isolation for weeks. My mind was racing and then when I almost gave up and was close to tears, a gentle voice in my head said "you have been studying about the benefits of the medicinal trees for a reason. It is time to apply what you have learnt." I sensed a ray of hope and I meditated. I called Amrid and gave him a chikoo stalk to boil with a few leaves of guava. The stalk of the Chikoo helps as anti viral and anti bacteria, while the leaves of guava help in reducing fever. I prayed that night that the medicine would work and Amrid would be back at work. Sure enough at 7.45 am the next day I saw the smiling face of Amrid. "It worked, it worked" he said with excitement. This gave me the confidence to continue.

After reviewing and studying the leaves, the idea of making infusions dawned on me. Tea for Two as the English say! Many great ideas have come from sipping cups of teas and infusions and *Volia*! I wanted to bring these helpful infusions to as many people as I could. Thus the concept of making a small, and useful tea table book was born. I called my Aunt Jo and requested her to help me put this together. So with her help I share all that I have learnt here at Mangaal.

I do hope the different infusions that I have put together will help you experience plant medicine. They work deeply on the mind and at an emotional level too. While you sip your infusion, imagine the healing fragrance wafting from the forest.

Like a wine connoisseur, smell the freshly brewed infusion, inhale the fragrance and take a small sip. Be aware of the tiny sip slowly moving around your palate and sliding down your throat. Close your eyes and experience the brewed water which contains the magic of the forest. Allow the leaves, soil and the air of the forest to penetrate into your well being, touching all that needs to heal.

So let's open the doors to the plant medicine world to explore and be guided by them. Before we venture into the forest infusions let understand how 'well being' works.

Cup of Tea

When the world is all at odds
And the mind is all at sea
Then cease the useless tedium
And brew a cup of tea

There is magic in its fragrance
There is solace in its taste
And then laden moments vanish
Somehow into space

And the world becomes a lovely thing!
There is beauty as you'll see
All because you briefly stopped
To brew a cup of tea.

Unknown artist

Wellbeing

Wellbeing, means different things to different people. For me wellbeing is an integration of physical and mental emotions. It is important to keep the physical body in shape but also the mind. Yoga and Pranayam is great for a flexible body but we also need to have a flexible mind. Our mind creates many thoughts which at times are chaotic. It has been said having a cup of tea makes our mind, thoughts and emotions calmer and creates a feeling of tranquillity.

The whole idea of making a cup of tea is do it mindfully; it is almost like a mediation.

Before I pluck the leaves, I thank the tree and the plant for allowing me to do so, telling them that many would benefit from it. Chanting the universal sound OM, I gently and carefully pluck the leaves that were calling out to me. The flowers, used in my infusions, are freshly fallen ... never plucked.

The days where you are anxious and cannot see clarity; sip a cup of Grounding, Balancing and Calming infusion. The Vetiver has the ability to do just that or you can try some mint.

A lot of times I use Elaichi, mint and saffron to help calm myself. Here is a recipe for you to try. While my pot of water is boiling I add a couple of eliachi, some crushed mint and a few strands of saffron. Soothing and calming! You could add honey if you wish.

Remember when you hold the cup of goodness in your hands, to look down into the cup and thank the ingredients for calming you. Inhale deeply and allow the fragrance to carry into your body. Now take a sip and enjoy the moment!

Count your blessing

When upon life's billows
You are tempest tossed
When you are discouraged
Thinking all is lost
Count your many blessings
Name them one by one
And it will surprise you
What the lord has done
Count your blessings
Name them one by one
Count your blessings
See what god has done
Are you ever burdened
With a load of care?
Does the cross seem heavy
You are called to bear?
Count your many blessings
Every doubt will fly
And you will be singing
As the day goes by
When you look at others
With their lands and gold
Think that Christ has
Promised you his
Wealth untold

Count your many blessings
Money cannot buy
Your reward in heaven
Nor your home on high
So amid the conflict
Whether great or small
Do not be discouraged
God is over all
Count your many blessings
Angels will attend
Help and comfort give you

To your journeys end

Johnson Oatman Jr

Forest Meditation

In the wee hours of the morning, I woke up smelling the fresh breeze which brought the forests wet, grassy fragrance to my nose. I was still half asleep, enjoying the feeling of this comforting sensation in my body. I sat up and was engulfed in gratitude to the whole universe that had brought me here. With my eyes closed and spine straight I prepared myself for meditation. Running through my mind constantly was this thought.... I'm being guided.

Every leaf holds the energy of the entire forest which includes the plants, trees, soil, animals, birds, butterflies and all living creatures of the forest. It holds the pure energy of the sun, water and earth. Just like every cell in the human body holds a part of the universe in it or a Divine spark or God, or whatever else you believe in. Every drop of water is part of the ocean as it holds all the qualities in it.

Every leaf, flower, root and berries that have gone into making these infusions, hold the essence of the forest that it came from and will touch every cell in your body. Healing what needs to be healed. Here is the meditation the forest shared with me.

You and I are one
The monkeys and I are one
All the insects, birds and snakes
Lizards and I are one
The earth, the leaves and trees
And I are one
The forest and its land
And I are one

Remember that you are WATER
Cry. Cleanse. Flow. Let Go.
Remember that you are FIRE
Burn. Tame. Adapt. Ignite.
Remember that you are AIR
Observe. Breath. Focus. Decide.
Remember that you are EARTH
Ground. Give. Build. Heal.
Remember that you are SPIRIT
Connect. Listen. Know. Be Still.

Morning with Champa

The crackling sound of the branch and the baritone whooping sound of the Monkey woke me up one morning. I fumbled for my cell phone to have a look at the time as it was still dark outside. The cell phone showed 5:00 am, my eyes was still laden with sleep so I shut them and continued to hear the monkeys jumping from branch to branch with the rustling sound of the leaves in the background. A gentle breeze picked up the essence of the Chafa flower which wafted straight through my nose as if playing with my senses. I sat up in half lotus pose with my eyes shut and allowed my nose to meditate on the Chafa's essence. My senses swooned as I inhaled the gentle floral aroma with its sweet woody smell. I allowed it to flow through my body as if it was bathing me. I felt refreshed and bathed in happiness and joy. The woody earthy aroma grounded me and gave me the feeling I was home.

The Champa symbolises charm, grace, beauty, new beginnings, new life, birth, dedication and devotion. In Hawaii, when a young woman wears the flower behind her right ear, she is available for marriage, whilst wearing the flower in her left ear symbolises that she is already promised. Buddhists believe the flower symbolises immortality, as the tree still blooms even when it's uprooted. For the Mayans, it symbolises life and birth.

Infusion made with Champa brings out the essence of love and a renewal of life.

For the infusion we need two Champa flowers. Take only the petals. Bring a cup of water to a boil and place the petals in the water. Switch off the fire and cover for steeping. Strain and pour yourself a cup. Allow yourself to have your own experience with beautiful champa.

I Believe

I believe for every drop of rain that falls
A flower grows.
I believe somewhere in the darkest night
A candle glows.
I believe for any one that goes astray
Someone will come to show the way.
I believe, I believe, I believe
Above the storm
A smallest prayer will still be heard
I believe somewhere in the grace
Someone hears every word
Every time I hear a new born baby cry
Or touch a leaf, or see the sky
Then I know why I believe.

I Believe

This song says it all. I leave it to my readers to draw their own conclusions as to what life is. I hope your beliefs are based on experience, as it leads us on the path we are meant to be on. There is a force much greater than us that knows what is best for us. Have faith in yourself and believe in what you feel strongly, no matter what others say. They are not in your shoes or on your journey.

To help having more faith in yourself and building confidence, here's an infusion that really helps. Make yourself a delicious cup of Champa infusion with a hint of cinnamon. This infusion brings with it the essence of stability and warmth.

Recipe is for one person:

Petals from one champa flower

1 small stick of cinnamon

Boil a cup of water with the cinnamon stick. Lovingly add the petals and switch off the flame. Cover and allow the flower to steep in the cinnamon water. Strain and pour yourself a magical cuppa.

The next forest infusion I would like to introduce is one made with Vetiver and Allspice. This is a combination of roots with leaves.

A Root with Leaf

The roots bring you grounding while the leaves bring you calmness and balance.

GROUNDING, BALANCING AND CALMING INFUSIONS

Allspice and Vetiver leaves were chosen for their ability to boost immunity, for anti viral, good blood circulation and enhance good digestion. The Vetiver root has grounding, balancing and a calming effect on us.

The leaf helps us to understand balance. The stem is balanced by the leaves, and it nourishes the plant. The root holds the plant firmly in the ground so it is able to weather through all kinds of seasons.

I recommend thanking all the plants that have gone into brewing this herbal infusion for you. Love and gratitude takes us a long way in life, by doing this small gesture we keep ourselves humble and thankful.

How to brew your infusion?

While still feeling gratitude, start boiling the water for your infusion. Place the leaves of the Allspice and roots of Vetiver into the boiling water and switch off the heat. Let it steep for ten minutes, this allows it to release its magical healing properties into the water.

Hold this cup of warm tea in your hand and look into the cup, thanking everything responsible for this superb infusion. Take a deep breath of the warm vapour from your cup. Smell the aroma and smile. Feel happy about this warmth. Savour a small sip and allow yourself to feel the warmth of the woody essence of Vetiver and the spices from the All Spice leaf. Allow the mind to be aware of how this infusion is making you feel.

Monkeying Around

Early one morning at the Mangaal plantation, the monkeys were at play once more. My attention was caught by the rustling of the leaves, it was as if the branches were miming a shamanic rattle. As I paid close attention to it I saw a long thing hanging down like a rope, on taking a closer look I realised it was a tail! The monkeys were frisky and were frog leaping from one branch to another. Eventually, they all settled down on two large trees and started feasting on the leaves. By now my curiosity had increased and I was behaving just like them! I started peering through my window and watching them in wonderment, in the way they often do when they see us humans. I saw them feasting and gobbling on Jamoon and Guava leaves.

"These are smart beings and know what is good for them." On doing some research i found the following.

The research revealed that Guava leaves are good for a number of different symptoms, cough, cold, fights cancer; helps lose weight besides being great for diabetes. The Jamboon leaves are anti bacterial, good for diabetes, cough and good for bad breath. I now present to you the monkeys recommendation.... Jamboon and Guava infusion!

Jamboon –Guava infusion

1 tsp jamboon leaves

1 tsp guava leaves

2 cups of water

Boil the above ingredients with two cups of water till the water reduces to half the quantity. Savour and sip away slowly allowing the leaves to work its magic.

BLOOM
IN YOUR OWN TIME

The Periwinkle story

Being a healer I met Shamans on my journey. I now decided to venture out on my own Shamanism path. I had seen a few documentaries where the Shaman walks in the forest and gets drawn towards a particular plant or tree. He then connects with the plant to understand its properties.

The environment here was perfect; the scene was ready for *'moi'* to experience her own shamanism. One morning in March, I sat in meditation in my warm cosy room and asked the plant energy to guide me towards the appropriate plant for my first experience. *Voila*! The Periwinkle popped up. So I walked up to the plant and connected with it, sitting beside it I closed my eyes and focused on my breathing. My mind and breath slowed down as I felt a beautiful golden energy encompassing me. Telepathically, it was communicated to me to rub the Periwinkle leaf in the centre of both my palms. This was a way of initiating and connecting me to all other plant spirits. For my first experience the energies had chosen the Periwinkle for me.

This purple flower brings love and joy when eaten raw. It energises the hearts centre. A gateway was shown to me where the energy felt more like a protection. The purple flower helps you to go beyond the Self. To understand who you really are… the loveable and happy person you always were. The leaves when eaten give stability and balance. As I chewed upon the leaf I did feel a sense of balance.. many would say it is psychosomatic but I believe in what I experienced. The plant also gave me a sound to activate energy specially pertaining to Periwinkle … 'Hmmm' like the buzzing sound of the bee.

Periwinkle is a dainty little flower commonly found in gardens in hues of purple, pink and white. It's also known as Sada Bahar the flower that blooms and is always packed with goodness. The leaves are used for combating diabetes. This petite flower symbolises friendship, serenity and calmness. It aids in healing depression, relaxes the muscles, helps in releasing fluid retention, and best for diabetes. Now we move on to the Periwinkle flower and leaf infusion.

Sada Bahar Infusion:

1 Periwinkle flower

2 Periwinkle leaves

1 cup water

Boil the flower and leaf together with one cup of water. Strain and sip. The leaf can be eaten raw on an empty stomach for those who suffer from diabetes, first thing in the morning.

The Flower Power

Flowers on the tree indicate many things and even predict the supply of food during the summer. When a flower blooms in spring it means that there would be sufficient fruit in summer. It also suggests there would be adequate water supply for crops during winter. During the 'hunter and gatherer' times people would look at the colours of flowers, which acted as a guide to finding ripe fruits.

Flowers are an important part of our culture. They are prominently used in our holy places, for weddings, festivals and for gifting. Besides this they are used for making medicines, perfumes and essences. Their seeds and other parts are used for various products and to put in food. Some of these seeds are greatly prized and are protected for their intrinsic value.

Flowers have been prominent in Vedic times for healing.

In ancient times the purple bauhinia was effective in treating cough, inflammation, piles and wounds.

The Arabian jasmine was used to treat eye diseases, poisoning and skin issues.

The beautiful Marigold flower represented patience, good fortune and was considered auspicious because of its colour.

Most Eastern faiths believe in the Lotus as a symbol of purity of life, fertility and youth. The Hindus believe that one should perform duties without attachment to the world to get *Moksh.*

Aak flower(calotropis gigantean) and dhatura flower are used at Maha Shivratri to honour Lord Shiva. Aak is similar to Shiva's personality as the flower needs to be handled properly otherwise It is poisonous! But used correctly it is medicine.

The Bach flower remedy. (information from web MD by Mary Jo Dilonardo)

In the 1900's Edward Bach, a medical doctor and a Homeopath believed in the healing powers of flowers. These were mostly flowers of wild plants which he then diluted. He believed that body could cure itself. These flower extracts work only on emotions and not symptoms. Bach believed that healing the negative emotions would help heal the person emotionally. In his system there are 38 remedies, each of them addresses a specific negative emotion. The emotions are largely grouped into the following which cause illness:

1. Fear
2. Uncertainty
3. Lack of interest in the present circumstances
4. Loneliness
5. Oversensitivity to influences and ideas
6. Sadness or despair
7. Care for others at the expense of self

I am quite sure most of us resonate to these above emotions and their effect on our health. Emotions also influence our eating habits.

Which flowers to use to make infusion from home?

Champa flower: infusion help in uplifting emotions.

Rose flower : anti depressant, anti spasmodic, anti bacterial and antiseptic.

Red Hibiscus flower: full of antioxidant, boosts liver, fights bacteria, prevents cancer.

Bougainville flower: anti cancer, anti diabetic, anti inflammatory, fertility control, anti microbial.

Marigold flower: soothes mucus in throat, anti oxidant, Vitamin A, antiseptic, anti inflammatory, heals the skin.

Jasmine flower: relaxes and relieves stress.

Parijat flower: anti pyretic/ fever, treats arthritic knee and sciatic pain, dry cough, immunity booster, treats Malaria.

Coffee & All Spice Infusion

The nearest to a tea leaf is a coffee leaf. Yes you heard right, the coffee leaf. I asked the women folk at the Mangaal plantation to collect some coffee leaves for me. I dehydrated and crushed these leaves and to my amazement it was true, the coffee leaf did taste like tea. Wanting to add some flavour and a little intensity, I thought of the woody and special flavours of the All Spice. This infusion has the richness of the coffee leaf and the potency of the Allspice.

The coffee leaves help in relieving constipation, depression, acute asthma, fatigue, hangover and migraine. The qualities of the Allspice are that they are an anti oxidant, fights cancer, anti viral, antiseptic, antifungal and is a sedative. The versatile Allspice leaves are also used for indigestion, cough, colds, high BP, pain reliever, increases blood circulation, boost immunity, anti viral and anti inflammatory.

The coffee leaf is used as a cleanser. In ancient times it was used as a medicine to keep the dark energies away but also helps in grounding. Its strong earthy, bold fragrance reminds me of the strength we have within. The coffee beans help us to connect to our higher Self....you and your strength. While the leaves help us to be firmly balanced on earth and therefore in centring one self. Once again, I used my intuition to connect with the coffee plant as it called out to me. The plant gave me the sound "Aaa loo haa" to chant while I was plucking its leaves. It basically gave me permission and also its blessings.

The recipe,

50 dry leaves of coffee

10 dry leaves of Allspice

Set your tea pot to boil with two cups of water. As you water comes to a boil, add a quarter teaspoon of each leaf and then allow it to steep for 5 minutes. Strain and sip.

Leaf medicine

Leaves speak of balance. A plant manages to stay upright with the help of its leaves. They not only make chlorophyll but also absorb light energy. Chlorophyll has anti oxidant properties and boost red blood cells. The leaves contain a mix of vitamins, minerals, proteins and anti oxidant. It is good for the heart, blood sugar, immune system and repairs cells.

Betel leaf, bay leaf, papaya leaf, guava leaf, chikko leaf, mango leaf, bougainville leaf all have medicinal value.

Bay leaf: diabetes, cancer, stomach related issues,

Betel leaf: anti oxidant, manages diabetes, heart, intestinal worms, cholesterol, contains vitamin C, thiamine, niacin, riboflavin, carotene and calcium.

Papaya leaf: treats fever, dengue fever, reduces inflammation, prevents cancer, rich in enzymes like papain and chymopapin and increases platelet count. Papain helps in breaking down protein, great for reducing pain, fever, swelling, fluid retention, digestive, removes parasitic worms.

Chiko leaf: great to get fever down.

Food of the Forest

My experience with medicinal plants and herbs at Mangaal found their way into my daily diet.

I look at my vegetables and fruits with great appreciation and gratitude. Being a grower myself I enjoy the fruits of labour immensely. There is something about growing your own food and cooking it. It tastes different.

The ancients would recite a prayer and ask forgiveness to the plant before plucking it. With humble gratitude they would pluck those fruits and vegetables that are required for the day but no more.

Being a healer too and having worked with people with regard to their health and emotion I understood the innate wisdom our body habours. Our body knows how to repair itself and gives us signs as to when and what to eat.

My knowledge on this has been purely experiential. My curiosity was tickled by my mother in law. While cooking, she would be very particular as to when to bhuno/brown the jeera or add green chillies or garlic. I noticed it was the sequence with which the masalas were put in that would enhance its flavour. As a result, I use very little masala in my cooking, so that the flavour of the vegetables are amplified. Generally, I steam or roast my vegetables. While preparing a dish, I usually listen to some cheerful music or jazz. This puts me in a happy mood for cooking. Putting all my awareness into chopping the vegetables I enjoy the aromas of ghee or coconut oil sizzling and hissing as I throw in the other ingredients. I stick my nose over the steaming dishes to get the correct fragrance of that particular dish.

The beautiful aroma of warm ghee with dash of hing would trigger childhood memories and sometimes the roasted jeera in ghee could conjure up hunger instantly for me. I found myself asking my body what it needs today and at this particular time. Sometimes I would feel like a lemony sour and spicy food and sometimes lots of green raw salad. My body strongly indicates what it craves and needs so I go with its flow. Every day I experimented with what vegetables I had bought to eat and how to cook it.

You can write your own journal which will help you understand your needs better. I have shared my first day's journal with you and how I interpreted it.

DAY 1 in 20-11-2019

I was drawn to lots of green leafy vegetables like spinach, bathuwa and methi leaves. While putting them in my shopping bag I visualised how I was going to cook them. Maybe steaming them with garlic, fresh haldi, some green chillies and finishing up with a squeeze of lime. Next, I picked up mooli with their leaves to make a light soup with burnt garlic and dash of freshly ground pepper. I found myself being attracted to fresh raw haldi, ginger and some fruits such as Persimmon and yellow Apples.

If you analyse the food I chose, it meant that my body was craving iron. This is found in all greens and chilli. The lemon contains Vitamin C which enhances the vegetables to absorb iron better. Radish too called out to me as it is full of calcium and potassium,that was deficient in my body. Turmeric has curcumin which is great for the heart, it is an anti oxidant and great to get rid of anxiety ....which I was feeling. Persimmon beckoned me and on analysing its properties I realised it contains vitamins A &C and manganese which was greatly beneficial for the leg cramps I was suffering from. Apples are rich in fibre and are an anti oxidant, it lowers the risk of heart attacks, diabetes, promotes good gut and brain health.

The Road Not Taken

Two roads diverged in a Yellow wood,
And sorry I could not travel both
And be one traveller, long I stood
And looked down one as far as I could
To where it bent in the undergrowth;

Then took the other, as just as fair,
And having perhaps the better claim,
Because it was grassy and wanted wear;
Though as for that the passing there
Had worn them really about the same,

And both that morning equally lay
In leaves no step had trodden black.
Oh, I kept the first for another day!
Yet knowing how way leads on to way,
I doubted if I should ever come back.

I shall be telling this with a sigh
Somewhere ages and ages hence:
Two roads diverged in a wood, and i-
I took the one less travelled by,
And that has made all the difference.

By Robert Frost

I hope Robert Frost has inspired you to have courage and walk your path. Most often it will be the path not explored but it will make all the difference in your life. To help you pluck up courage and move on, I have chosen Lemon Balm Mint and Basil infusion for you.

Lemon Balm Mint & Basil Infusion

2 stems of Lemon Balm Mint

2 stems of Basil

1 stem of mint

Slice of Lemon for garnish

200 ml of water

Set your pot to boil, while boiling add in the leaves and allow to brew for 5 minutes. Switch off the heat and allow the infusion to steep. Pour mixture into your favourite cup and remember you have the courage to walk your path. Thank the leaves and the plant for supporting you in your journey.

The Root Power

One morning, on my round of the plantation I saw our farm hands transplanting. So I joined them. This was done inside a large shed which gave the feeling of openness. Mini 'green grow bags' dotted the place.

'Perfect' I thought to myself. How wonderful it would be if we converted this shed into a nursery? The infinity sign showed up in my minds imagination. So we began to place the grow bags in an infinity design. These were bags full of Japanese mint, pepper mint, spear mint but the magical one was Vaikhand., While shifting the grow bags around, I drew closer to the plant. I felt my senses heighten and I asked Amrid, "what plant is this?" "This is Vaikundh, a plant that only grows where the energy is right. The root of this plant is medicinal," replied Amrid.

We often use the term 'root' in our daily vocabulary such as "I am back to my roots". Or I want to find my roots or what is the root cause of the problem without thinking deeper in to its actual meaning. The roots do just that, take you deeper.

In my early morning meditation I was made aware of Kabir Das, a Sufi poet. He often wrote poems based on potters, weavers etc. For example the potter makes many beautiful objects though different, they all have a common thread...mud. A drop of water has no awareness that it holds the same qualities as the ocean, even though it's made of same substance. In the same way, we are all a part of the universe with all its qualities. Just like a drop of water we too need to develop the awareness. Let us journey with the roots to find ourselves... the knowledge we already have but we need to develop an access to get to it.

May the root infusions of vetiver, haldi, mango ginger, ginger and vaikhand bring out your well being and help you to find your roots. The vaikhand is a plant which is much like the Amethyst crystal, a master healer for most ailments.

The Root Infusion

Vaikhand root infusion.

This master root infusion aids in sharpening memory, cognition, intelligence, mental abilities, the vocal cord, stomach issues, liver, lung, anxiety, digestion, inflammation, arthritis and asthma.

1 tsp of vaikhand powder or 125mg

1 cup water/milk

1 tsp Honey

Boil the water or milk with 1 tsp of the powder. Add in the honey and sip away.

This is to be drunk twice a day after meals.

The same powder of the vaikhand root can be mixed with water and made into a paste and applied on the forehead to lessen a headache, heavy head or dull head.

Another Root -Vetiver infusion

This helps in balancing the mind and body specially when under stress. Also, anxiety, depression, emotional out bursts and basically is great for those who require grounding.

1 tsp dry vetiver root

1 tsp dry lemon balm

1 tsp dry all spice leaf

Boil the above ingredients with 1 cup of water. Strain and sip slowly.

The roots play a vital role in the plant, besides holding the plant or tree to the soil firmly, it nourishes them with minerals too. The root also communicates with other fellow trees via mycorrhizal network, by sending distress signals of insect invasion, drought, or danger. They even send signals to other roots to help replenish the lack of certain minerals they need. The soil is made up of all the properties that are within us and plants.

AS ONE DOOR SHUTS - ANOTHER OPENS

I knew it was time for me to leave Mangaal as I had done all that I could at the plantation. The forests had played an important role in my journey. Their touch changed me for life. Armed with love, knowledge and experience it was time for me to move on to my new destination where I could share what I had learnt and experienced here.

As we reach at the end of this book I would like to share this beautiful poem with you..

The Oak Tree

A mighty wind blew night and day.
It stole the oak tree's leaves away.
Then snapped its boughs and pulled its bark
Until the oak was tired and stark.
But still the oak tree held its ground
While other trees fell all around.
The weary wind gave up and spoke,
"How can you still be standing, Oak?"
The Oak tree said, "I know that you
Can break each branch of mine into two,
Carry every leaf away,
Shake my limbs, and make me sway.
But I have roots stretched in the earth,
Growing stronger since my birth.
You'll never touch them, for you see,
They are deepest part of me.
Until today, I wasn't sure
Of just how much I could endure.
But now I've found, with thanks to you,
I'm stronger than I ever knew."

Johnny Ray Ryder Jr.

Advice from Maria Sabina, Mexican healer and poet.

"Heal yourself with the light of the sun and the rays of the moon. With the sound of the river and the waterfall. With the swaying of the sea and the fluttering of birds. Heal yourself with mint, neem, and eucalyptus. Sweeten with lavender, rosemary, and chamomile. Hug yourself with the cocoa bean and a hint of cinnamon. Put love in tea instead of sugar and drink it looking at the stars. Heal yourself with the kisses that the wind gives you and the hugs of the rain Stand strong with your bare feet on the ground and with everything that comes from it. Be smarter every day by listening to your intuition, looking at the world with your forehead. Jump, dance, sing, so that you live happier. Heal yourself, with beautiful love, and always remember ... you are the medicine."